THE RUBAIYÁT OF
OMAR KHAYYÁM

RUBÁIYÁT
OF
OMAR KHAYYÁM

RENDERED INTO ENGLISH VERSE BY
Edward Fitzgerald

FIRST AND FIFTH VERSIONS

WITH DRAWINGS BY
Edmund J. Sullivan

NEW YORK
Illustrated Editions Company
220 FOURTH AVENUE

Contents

RUBÁIYÁT OF
OMAR KHAYYAM

OMAR KHAYYÁM,

THE ASTRONOMER-POET OF PERSIA.

OMAR KHAYYÁM was born at Naishápúr in Khorassán in the latter half of our Eleventh, and died within the First Quarter of our Twelfth Century. The Slender Story of his Life is curiously twined about that of two other very considerable Figures in their Time and Country: one of whom tells the Story of all Three. This was Nizám ul Mulk, Vizier to Alp Arslan the Son, and Malik Shah the Grandson, of Toghrul Beg the Tartar, who had wrested Persia from the feeble Successor of Mahmúd the Great, and founded that Seljukian Dynasty which finally roused Europe into the Crusades. This Nizám ul Mulk, in his *Wasiyat*—or *Testament* —which he wrote and left as a Memorial for future Statesmen —relates the following, as quoted in the *Calcutta Review,* No. 59, from Mirkhond's History of the Assassins.

" 'One of the greatest of the wise men of Khorassán was the Imám Mowaffak of Naishápúr, a man highly honored and reverenced,—may God rejoice his soul; his illustrious years exceeded eighty-five, and it was the universal belief that every boy who read the Koran or studied the traditions in his presence, would assuredly attain to honor and happiness. For this cause did my father send me from Tús to Naishápúr with Abd-us-samad, the doctor of law, that I might employ myself in study and learning under the guidance of that illustrious teacher. Towards me he ever turned an eye of favor and kindness, and as his pupil I felt for him extreme affection and devotion, so that I passed four years in his service. When I first came there, I found two other pupils of mine own age newly arrived, Hakim Omar Khayyám, and the ill-fated Ben Sabbáh. Both were endowed with sharpness of wit and the highest natural powers; and we three formed a close friendship together. When the Imám rose from his lectures, they used to join me, and we repeated to each other the lessons we had heard. Now Omar was a native of Naishápúr, while Hasan Ben Sabbáh's father was one Ali, a man of austere life and practise, but heretical in his creed and doctrine. One day Hasan said to me and to Khayyám, "It is a universal belief that the pupils of the Imám Mowaffak will attain to fortune. Now, even if we *all* do not attain thereto, without doubt one of us will; what then shall be our mutual pledge and bond?" We answered, "Be it what you please." "Well," he said, "let us make a vow, that to whomsoever this fortune falls, he shall share it equally with the rest, and reserve no pre-eminence for himself." "Be it so," we both replied, and on those terms we mutually pledged our words. Years rolled on, and I went from Khorassán to Transoxiana, and wandered to Ghazni and Cabul; and when I returned, I was invested with office, and rose to be administrator of affairs during the Sultanate of Sultan Alp Arslán.'

"He goes on to state, that years passed by, and both his old school-friends found him out, and came and claimed a share in his good fortune, according to the school-day vow. The Vizier was generous and kept his word. Hasan demanded a place in the government, which the Sultan granted at the Vizier's request; but discontented with a gradual rise, he plunged into the maze of intrigue of an oriental court, and, failing in a base attempt to supplant his benefactor, he was disgraced and fell. After many mishaps and wanderings, Hasan became the head of the Persian sect of the *Ismailians,* —a party of fanatics who had long murmured in obscurity, but rose to an evil eminence under the guidance of his strong and evil will. In A.D. 1090, he seized the castle of Alamút, in the province of Rúdbar, which lies in the mountainous tract south of the Caspian Sea; and it was from this mountain home he obtained that evil celebrity among the Crusaders as the OLD MAN OF THE MOUNTAINS, and spread terror through the Mohammedan world; and it is yet disputed whether the word *Assassin,* which they have left in the language of modern Europe as their dark memorial, is derived from the *hashish,* or opiate of hemp-leaves (the Indian *bhang*), with which they maddened themselves to the sullen pitch of oriental desperation, or from the name of the founder of the dynasty, whom we have seen in his quiet collegiate days, at Naishápúr. One of the countless victims of the Assassin's dagger was Nizám ul Mulk himself, the old school-boy friend.[1]

"Omar Khayyám also came to the Vizier to claim his share; but not to ask for title or office. 'The greatest boon you can confer on me,' he said, 'is to let me live in a corner under the shadow of your fortune, to spread wide the advantages of Science, and pray for your long life and prosperity.' The Vizier tells us, that when he found Omar was really sincere in his refusal, he pressed him no further, but granted him a yearly pension of 1200 *mithkáls* of gold from the treasury of Naishápúr.

[1] Some of Omar's Rubáiyát warn us of the danger of Greatness, the instability of Fortune, and while advocating Charity to all Men, recommending us to be too intimate with none. Attár makes Nizám-ul-Mulk use the very words of his friend Omar [Rub. xxviii.], "When Nizám-ul-Mulk was in the Agony (of Death) he said, 'Oh God! I am passing away in the hand of the wind.'"

"At Naishápúr thus lived and died Omar Khayyám, 'busied,' adds the Vizier, 'in winning knowledge of every kind, and especially in Astronomy, wherein he attained to a very high pre-eminence. Under the Sultanate of Malik Shah, he came to Merv, and obtained great praise for his proficiency in science, and the Sultan showered favors upon him.'

"When the Malik Shah determined to reform the calendar, Omar was one of the eight learned men employed to do it; the result was the *Jaláli* era (so called from *Jalál-ud-din,* one of the king's names)—'a computation of time,' says Gibbon, 'which surpasses the Julian, and approaches the accuracy of the Gregorian style.' He is also the author of some astronomical tables, entitled 'Zíji-Maliksháhí,' and the French have lately republished and translated an Arabic Treatise of his on Algebra.

"His Takhallus or poetical name (Khayyám) signifies a Tent-maker, and he is said to have at one time exercised that trade, perhaps before Nizám-ul-Mulk's generosity raised him to independence. Many Persian poets similarly derive their names from their occupations; thus we have Attár, 'a druggist,' Assár, 'an oil presser,' etc.[1] Omar himself alludes to his name in the following whimsical lines:—

" 'Khayyám, who stitched the tents of science,
    Has fallen in grief's furnace and been suddenly burned;
    The shears of Fate have cut the tent ropes of his life,
    And the broker of Hope has sold him for nothing!'

"We have only one more anecdote to give of his Life, and that relates to the close; it is told in the anonymous preface which is sometimes prefixed to his poems; it has been printed in the Persian in the Appendix to Hyde's *Veterum Persarum*

[1] Though all these, like our Smiths, Archers, Millers, Fletchers, etc., may simply retain the Surname of an hereditary calling.

Religio, p. 499; and D'Herbelot alludes to it in his Bibliothèque, under *Khiam*.[1]—

"'It is written in the chronicles of the ancients that this
King of the Wise, Omar Khayyám, died at Naishápúr in the
year of the Hegira, 517 (A.D. 1123); in science he was un-
rivaled,—the very paragon of his age. Khwájah Nizámi of
Samarcand, who was one of his pupils, relates the following
story: "I often used to hold conversations with my teacher,
Omar Khayyám, in a garden; and one day he said to me,
'My tomb shall be in a spot where the north wind may scatter
roses over it.' I wondered at the words he spake, but I knew
that his were no idle words.[2] Years after, when I chanced to
revisit Naishápúr, I went to his final resting-place, and lo!
it was just outside a garden, and trees laden with fruit
stretched their boughs over the garden wall, and dropped
their flowers upon his tomb, so that the stone was hidden
under them."'"

Thus far—without fear of Trespass— from the *Calcutta Review.* The writer of it, on reading in India this story of Omar's
Grave, was reminded, he says, of Cicero's Account of finding
Archimedes' Tomb at Syracuse, buried in grass and weeds. I
think Thorwaldsen desired to have roses grow over him; a

[1] "Philosophe Musulman qui a vécu en Odeur de Sainteté dans sa Religion, vers
la Fin du premier et le Commencement du second Siècle," no part of which, ex-
cept the "Philosophe," can apply to our Khayyám.

[2] The Rashness of the Words, according to D'Herbelot, consisted in being so
opposed to those in the Korán: "No Man knows where he shall die."—This story of
Omar reminds me of another so naturally—and when one remembers how wide
of his humble mark the noble sailor aimed—so pathetically told by Captain Cook
—not by Doctor Hawksworth—in his Second Voyage (i. 374). When leaving
Ulietea, "Oreo's last request was for me to return. When he saw he could not
obtain that promise, he asked the name of my *Marai* (burying-place). As strange a
question as this was, I hesitated not a moment to tell him 'Stepney'; the parish in
which I live when in London. I was made to repeat it several times over till they
could pronounce it; and then 'Stepney Marai no Toote' was echoed through an
hundred mouths at once. I afterwards found the same question had been put to
Mr. Forster by a man on shore; but he gave a different, and indeed more proper
answer, by saying, 'No man who used the sea could say where he should be
buried.'"

wish religiously fulfilled for him to the present day, I believe. However, to return to Omar.

Though the Sultan "shower'd Favors upon him," Omar's Epicurean Audacity of Thought and Speech caused him to be regarded askance in his own Time and Country. He is said to have been especially hated and dreaded by the Súfis, whose Practise he ridiculed, and whose Faith amounts to little more than his own, when stript of the Mysticism and formal recognition of Islamism under which Omar would not hide. Their Poets, including Háfiz, who are (with the exception of Firdausi) the most considerable in Persia, borrowed largely, indeed, of Omar's material, but turning it to a mystical Use more convenient to Themselves and the People they addressed; a People quite as quick of Doubt as of Belief; as keen of Bodily sense as of Intellectual; and delighting in a cloudy composition of both, in which they could float luxuriously between Heaven and Earth, and this World and the Next, on the wings of a poetical expression, that might serve indifferently for either. Omar was too honest of Heart as well of Head for this. Having failed (however mistakenly) of finding any Providence but Destiny, and any World but This, he set about making the most of it; preferring rather to soothe the Soul through the Senses into Acquiescence with Things as he saw them, than to perplex it with vain disquietude after what they *might* be. It has been seen, however, that his Worldly Ambition was not exorbitant; and he very likely takes a humorous or perverse pleasure in exalting the gratification of Sense above that of the Intellect, in which he must have taken great delight, although it failed to answer the Questions in which he, in common with all men, was most vitally interested.

For whatever Reason, however, Omar as before said, has never been popular in his own Country, and therefore has been but scantily transmitted abroad. The MSS. of his Poems,

mutilated beyond the average Casualties of Oriental Trans-
cription, are so rare in the East as scarce to have reacht West-
ward at all, in spite of all the acquisitions of Arms and Science.
There is no copy at the India House, none at the Bibliothèque
Nationale of Paris. We know but of one in England: No. 140
of the Ouseley MSS. at the Bodleian, written at Shiráz, A.D.
1460. This contains but 158 Rubáiyát. One in the Asiatic So-
ciety's Library at Calcutta (of which we have a Copy), contains (and yet incomplete) 516, though swelled to that by all
kinds of Repetition and Corruption. So Von Hammer speaks
of *his* Copy as containing about 200, while Dr. Sprenger cata-
logues the Lucknow MS. at double that number.[1] The Scribes,
too, of the Oxford and Calcutta MSS. seem to do their Work
under a sort of Protest; each beginning with a Tetrastich
(whether genuine or not), taken out of its alphabetical order;
the Oxford with one of Apology; the Calcutta with one of
Expostulation, supposed (says a Notice prefixed to the MS.)
to have arisen from a Dream, in which Omar's mother asked
about his future fate. It may be rendered thus:—

"Oh Thou who burn'st in Heart for those who burn
In Hell, whose fires thyself shall feed in turn,
How long be crying, 'Mercy on them, God!'
Why, who art Thou to teach, and He to learn?"

The Bodleian Quatrain pleads Pantheism by way of Justifi-
cation.

"If I myself upon a looser Creed
Have loosely strung the Jewel of Good deed,
Let this one thing for my Atonement plead:
That One for Two I never did misread."

[1] "Since this paper was written" (adds the Reviewer in a note), "we have met
with a Copy of a very rare Edition, printed at Calcutta in 1836. This contains 438
Tetrastichs, with an Appendix containing 54 others not found in some MSS."

The Reviewer,[1] to whom I owe the Particulars of Omar's Life, concludes his Review by comparing him with Lucretius, both as to natural Temper and Genius, and as acted upon by the Circumstances in which he lived. Both indeed were men of subtle, strong, and cultivated Intellect, fine Imagination, and Hearts passionate for Truth and Justice; who justly revolted from their Country's false Religion, and false, or foolish, Devotion to it; but who fell short of replacing what they subverted by such better *Hope* as others, with no better Revelation to guide them, had yet made a Law to themselves. Lucretius indeed, with such material as Epicurus furnished, satisfied himself with the theory of a vast machine fortuitously constructed, and acting by a Law that implied no Legislator; and so composing himself into a Stoical rather than Epicurean severity of Attitude, sat down to contemplate the mechanical drama of the Universe which he was part Actor in; himself and all about him (as in his own sublime description of the Roman Theater) discolored with the lurid reflex of the Curtain suspended between the Spectator and the Sun. Omar, more desperate, or more careless of any so complicated System as resulted in nothing but hopeless Necessity, flung his own Genius and Learning with a bitter or humorous jest into the general Ruin which their insufficient glimpses only served to reveal; and, pretending sensual pleasure, as the serious purpose of Life, only *diverted* himself with speculative problems of Deity, Destiny, Matter and Spirit, Good and Evil, and other such questions, easier to start than to run down, and the pursuit of which becomes a very weary sport at last!

With regard to the present Translation. The original Rubáiyát (as, missing an Arabic Guttural, these *Tetrastichs* are more musically called) are independent Stanzas, consist-

[1] Professor Cowell.

ing each of four Lines of equal, though varied, Prosody; sometimes *all* rhyming, but oftener (as here imitated) the third line a blank. Somewhat as in the Greek Alcaic, where the penultimate line seems to lift and suspend the Wave that falls over in the last. As usual with such kind of Oriental Verse, the Rubáiyát follow one another according to Alphabetic Rhyme—a strange succession of Grave and Gay. Those here selected are strung into something of an Eclogue, with perhaps a less than equal proportion of the "Drink and make-merry," which (genuine or not) recurs over-frequently in the Original. Either way, the Result is sad enough: saddest perhaps when most ostentatiously merry: more apt to move Sorrow than Anger toward the old Tentmaker, who, after vainly endeavoring to unshackle his Steps from Destiny, and to catch some authentic Glimpse of To-MORROW, fell back upon To-DAY (which has outlasted so many To-morrows!) as the only Ground he had got to stand upon, however momentarily slipping from under his Feet.

EDWARD J. FITZGERALD

I

Awake! for Morning in the Bowl of Night

Has flung the Stone that puts the Stars to Flight:

   And Lo! the Hunter of the East has caught

The Sultán's Turret in a Noose of Light.

II

Dreaming when Dawn's Left Hand was in the Sky

I heard a Voice within the Tavern cry,

   "Awake, my Little ones, and fill the Cup

Before Life's Liquor in its Cup be dry."

III

And, as the Cock crew, those who stood before

The Tavern shouted—"Open then the Door.

You know how little while we have to stay,

And, once departed, may return no more."

IV

Now the New Year reviving old Desires,

The thoughtful Soul to Solitude retires,

    Where the WHITE HAND OF MOSES on the Bough

Puts out, and Jesus from the Ground suspires.

EDMUND·J·SULLIVAN

V

Irám indeed is gone with all its Rose,

And Jamshýd's Sev'n-ring'd Cup where no one

knows;

But still the Vine her ancient Ruby yields,

And still a Garden by the Water blows.

VI

And David's Lips are lock't; but in divine

High piping Pélevi, with "Wine! Wine! Wine!

   Red Wine!"—the Nightingale cries to the Rose

That yellow Cheek of hers to'incarnadine.

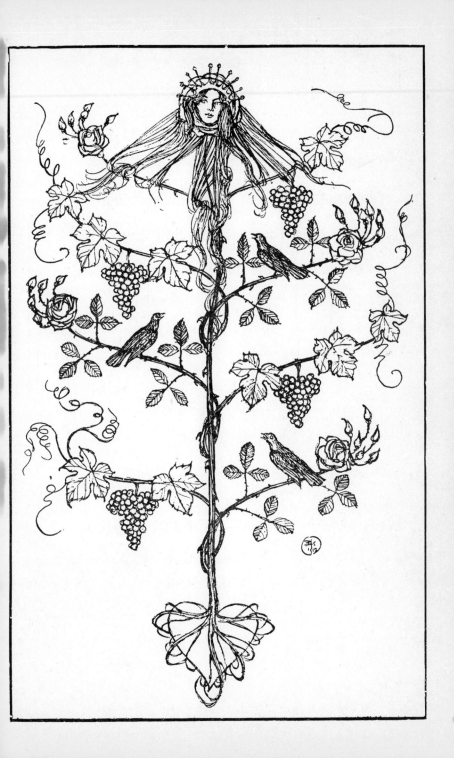

VII

Come, fill the Cup, and in the Fire of Spring

The Winter Garment of Repentance fling:

The Bird of Time has but a little way

To fly—and Lo! the Bird is on the Wing.

VIII

And look—a thousand Blossoms with the Day

Woke--–and a thousand scatter'd into Clay:

  And this first Summer Month that brings the

    Rose

Shall take Jamshýd and Kaikobád away.

IX

But come with old Khayyám, and leave the Lot

Of Kaikobád and Kaikhosrú forgot:

Let Rustum lay about him as he will,

Or Hátim Tai cry Supper—heed them not.

X

With me along some Strip of Herbage strown

That just divides the desert from the sown,

   Where name of Slave and Sultán scarce is known

And pity Sultán Máhmúd on his Throne.

XI

Here with a Loaf of Bread beneath the Bough,

A Flask of Wine, a Book of Verse—and Thou

Beside me singing in the Wilderness—

And Wilderness is Paradise enow.

EDMUND J. SULLIVAN

XII

"How sweet is mortal Sovranty!"—think some:

Others—"How blest the Paradise to come!"

Ah, take the Cash in hand and waive the Rest;

Oh, the brave Music of a *distant* Drum!

XIII

Look to the Rose that blows about us—"Lo,

Laughing," she says, "into the World I blow:

At once the silken Tassel of my Purse

Tear, and its Treasure on the Garden throw."

XIV

The Worldly Hope men set their Hearts upon

Turns Ashes—or it prospers; and anon,

   Like Snow upon the Desert's dusty Face

Lighting a little Hour or two—is gone.

XV

And those who husbanded the Golden Grain,

And those who flung it to the Winds like Rain,

   Alike to no such aureate Earth are turn'd

As, buried once, Men want dug up again.

LIE

EXPECTATION
of a
LORD'S RESURRECTION
the bodies of
ADAM
aged 930
and of his beloved wife EVE.

this stone is erected
in loving memory, by their son
CAIN.

EDMUND·J·SULLIVAN·

XVI

Think, in this batter'd Caravanserai

Whose Doorways are alternate Night and Day,

How Sultán after Sultán with his Pomp

Abode his Hour or two, and went his way.

XVII

They say the Lion and the Lizard keep

The Courts where Jamshýd gloried and drank

 deep:

 And Bahrám, that great Hunter—the Wild Ass

Stamps o'er his Head, and he lies fast asleep.

XVIII

I sometimes think that never blows so red

The Rose as where some buried Cæsar bled;

That every Hyacinth the Garden wears

Dropt in its Lap from some once lovely Head.

XIX

And this delightful Herb whose tender Green

Fledges the River's Lip on which we lean—

Ah, lean upon it lightly! for who knows

From what once lovely Lip it springs unseen!

Ah! my Belovéd, fill the Cup that clears

To-DAY of past Regrets and future Fears—

To-morrow?—Why, To-morrow I may be

Myself with Yesterday's Sev'n Thousand Years.

XXI

Lo! some we loved, the loveliest and the best

That Time and Fate of all their Vintage prest,

    Have drunk their Cup a Round or two before,

And one by one crept silently to Rest.

XXII

And we, that now make merry in the Room

They left, and Summer dresses in new Bloom,

    Ourselves must we beneath the Couch of Earth

Descend, ourselves to make a Couch—for whom?

HERE LIETH

HIS WIFE

OF THIS PARISH

EDMUND J SULLIVAN

XXIII

Ah, make the most of what we yet may spend,

Before we too into the Dust Descend;

  Dust into Dust, and under Dust, to lie,

Sans Wine, sans Song, sans Singer and—sans End!

EDMUND·J·SULLIVAN·

XXIV

Alike for those who for TO-DAY prepare,

And those that after a TO-MORROW stare,

    A Muezzín from the Tower of Darkness cries

"Fools! your Reward is neither Here nor There."

XXV

Why, all the Saints and Sages who discuss'd

Of the Two Worlds so learnedly, are thrust

   Like foolish Prophets forth; their Words to
     Scorn

Are scatter'd, and their Mouths are stopt with Dust

XXVI

Oh, come with old Khayyám, and leave the Wise

To talk; one thing is certain, that Life flies;

One thing is certain, and the Rest is Lies;

The Flower that once has blown for ever dies.

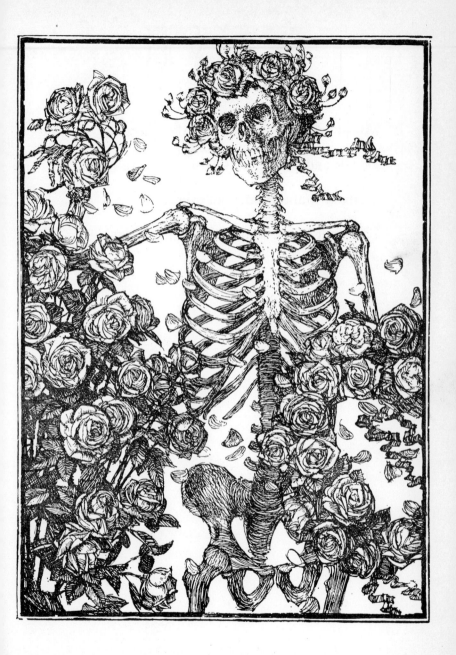

XXVII

Myself when young did eagerly frequent

Doctor and Saint, and heard great Argument

About it and about: but evermore

Came out by the same Door as in I went.

XXVIII

With them the Seed of Wisdom did I sow,

And with my own hand labour'd it to grow:

   And this was all the Harvest that I reap'd—

"I came like Water, and like Wind I go."

EDMUND·J·SULLIVAN

Into this Universe, and *why* not knowing,

Nor *whence,* like Water willy-nilly flowing:

  And out of it, as Wind along the Waste,

I know not *whither,* willy-nilly blowing.

XXX

What, without asking, hither hurried *whence?*

And, without asking, *whither* hurried hence!

　Another and another Cup to drown

The Memory of this Impertinence!

XXXI

Up from Earth's Centre through the seventh Gate

I rose, and on the Throne of Saturn sate,

    And many Knots unravel'd by the Road;

But not the Knot of Human Death and Fate.

XXXII

There was a Door to which I found no Key:

There was a Veil past which I could not see:

    Some little Talk awhile of ME and THEE

There seemed—and then no more of THEE and ME.

XXXIII

Then to the rolling Heav'n itself I cried,

Asking, "What Lamp had Destiny to guide

   Her little Children stumbling in the Dark?"

And—"A blind understanding!" Heav'n replied.

XXXIV

Then to this earthen Bowl did I adjourn

My Lip the secret Well of Life to learn:

   And Lip to Lip it murmur'd—"While you live,

Drink!—for once dead you never shall return."

XXXV

I think the Vessel, that with fugitive

Articulation answer'd, once did live,

   And merry-make; and the cold Lip I kiss'd

How many Kisses might it take—and give.

XXXVI

For in the Market-place, one Dusk of Day,

I watch'd the Potter thumping his wet Clay:

And with its all obliterated Tongue

It murmur'd—"Gently, Brother, gently, pray!"

XXXVII

Ah, fill the Cup:—what boots it to repeat

How Time is slipping underneath our Feet:

Unborn To-morrow and dead Yesterday,

Why fret about them if To-day be sweet!

XXXVIII

One Moment in Annihilation's Waste,

One moment, of the Well of Life to taste—

The Stars are setting, and the Caravan

Starts for the dawn of Nothing—Oh, make haste!

XXXIX

How long, how long, in infinite Pursuit

Of This and That endeavour and dispute?

  Better be merry with the fruitful Grape

Than sadden after none, or bitter, Fruit.

XL

You know, my Friends, how long since in my
    House
For a new Marriage I did make Carouse:
    Divorced old barren Reason from my Bed,
And took the Daughter of the Vine to Spouse.

XLI

For "Is" and "Is-not" though *with* Rule and Line,

And, "Up-and-Down" *without,* I could define,

   I yet in all I only cared to know,

Was never deep in anything but—Wine.

XLII

And lately, by the Tavern Door agape,

Came stealing through the Dusk an Angel Shape,

   Bearing a vessel on his Shoulder; and

He bid me taste of it; and 'twas—the Grape!

XLIII

The Grape that can with Logic absolute

The Two-and-Seventy jarring Sects confute:

The subtle Alchemist that in a Trice

Life's leaden Metal into Gold transmute

XLIV

The mighty Mahmúd, the victorious Lord,

That all the misbelieving and black Horde

Of Fears and Sorrows that infest the Soul

Scatters and slays with his enchanted Sword.

XLV

But leave the Wise to wrangle, and with me

The Quarrel of the Universe let be:

And, in some corner of the Hubbub coucht,

Make Game of that which makes as much of Thee.

XLVI

For in and out, above, about, below,

'Tis nothing but a Magic Shadow-show,

   Play'd in a Box whose Candle is the Sun,

Round which we Phantom Figures come and go.

XLVII

And if the Wine you drink, the Lip you press,

End in the Nothing all Things end in—Yes—

   Then fancy while Thou art, Thou art but what

Thou shalt be—Nothing—Thou shalt not be less.

XLVIII

While the Rose blows along the River Brink,

With old Khayyám the Ruby Vintage drink:

And when the Angel with his darker Draught

Draws up to thee—take that, and do not shrink.

XLIX

'Tis all a Chequer-board of Nights and Days

Where Destiny with Men for Pieces plays:

   Hither and thither moves, and mates, and slays,

And one by one back in the Closet lays.

L

The Ball no Question makes of Ayes and Noes,

But Right or Left as strikes the Player goes;

   And He that toss'd Thee down into the Field,

He knows about it all—HE knows—HE knows!

LI

The Moving Finger writes; and, having writ,

Moves on: nor all thy Piety nor Wit

    Shall lure it back to cancel half a Line,

Nor all thy Tears wash out a Word of it.

LII

And that inverted Bowl we call The Sky,

Whereunder crawling coop't we live and die,

 Lift not thy hands to *It* for help—for It

Rolls impotently on as Thou or I.

LIII

With Earth's first Clay They did the Last Man's
  knead,
And then of the Last Harvest sow'd the Seed:
  Yea, the first Morning of Creation wrote
What the Last Dawn of Reckoning shall read.

FINIS

written off
and
account closed
AΩ

LIV

I tell Thee this—When, starting from the Goal,

Over the shoulders of the flaming Foal

   Of Heav'n Parwín and Mushtarí they flung,

In my predestin'd Plot of Dust and Soul

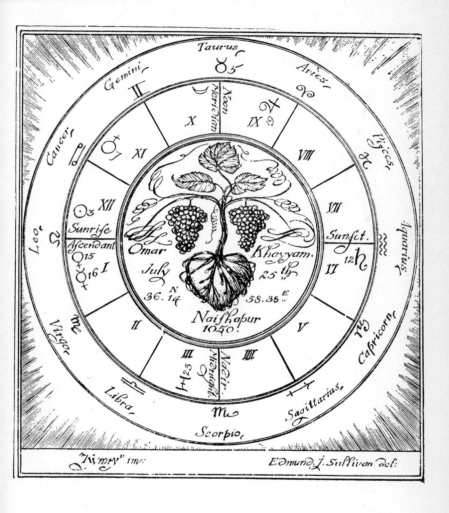

LV

The Vine had struck a Fibre; which about

It clings my Being—let the Súfi flout;

   Of my Base Metal may be filed a Key,

That shall unlock the Door he howls without.

LVI

And this I know: whether the one True Light,

Kindle to Love, or Wrath consume me quite,

   One Glimpse of It within the Tavern caught

Better than in the Temple lost outright.

EDMUND·J·SULLIVAN·

LVII

Oh Thou who didst with Pitfall and with Gin
Beset the Road I was to wander in,
   Thou wilt not with Predestination round
Enmesh me, and impute my Fall to Sin?

EDMUND J SULLIVAN

LVIII

Oh Thou, who Man of baser Earth didst make,

And who with Eden didst devise the Snake;

For all the Sin wherewith the Face of Man

Is blacken'd, Man's Forgiveness give—and take!

* * * * *

LIX

KUZA—NÁMA

Listen again. One Evening at the Close

Of Ramazán, ere the better Moon arose,

    In that old Potter's Shop I stood alone

With the clay Population round in Rows.

LX

And strange to tell, among that Earthen Lot

Some could articulate, while others not:

And suddenly one more impatient cried—

"Who *is* the Potter, pray, and who the Pot?"

EDMUND·J·SULLIVAN·

LXI

Then said another—"Surely not in vain

My substance from the common Earth was ta'en,

That He who subtly wrought me into Shape

Should stamp me back to common Earth again."

LXII

Another said—"Why, ne'er a peevish Boy

Would break the Bowl from which he drank in

    Joy;

  Shall He that *made* the Vessel in pure Love

And Fansy, in an after Rage destroy!"

LXIII

None answer'd this; but after Silence spake
A Vessel of a more ungainly Make:
  "They sneer at me for leaning all awry;
What? did the Hand then of the Potter shake?"

LXIV

Said one—"Folks of a surly Tapster tell,

And daub his Visage with the Smoke of Hell;

   They talk of some strict Testing of us—Pish!

He's a Good Fellow, and 'twill all be well."

EDMUND· J·SULLIVAN·

LXV

Then said another with a long-drawn Sigh,

"My Clay with long oblivion is gone dry:

But, fill me with the old familiar Juice,

Methinks I might recover by-and-bye!"

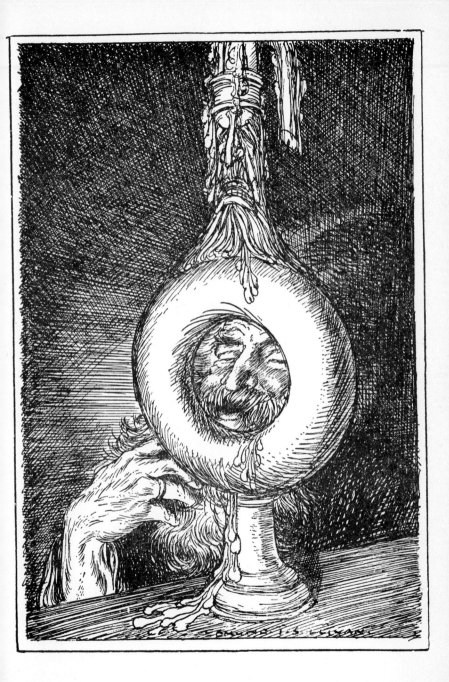

LXVI

So, while the Vessels one by one were speaking,

One spied the little Crescent all were seeking:

    And then they jogg'd each other, "Brother!

        Brother!

Hark to the Porter's Shoulder-knot a-creaking!"

      *   *   *   *   *

LXVII

Ah, with the Grape my fading Life provide,

And wash my Body whence the life has died,

And in a Windingsheet of Vineleaf wrapt,

So bury me by some sweet Gardenside.

EDMUND·J·SULLIVAN

LXVIII

That ev'n my buried Ashes such a Snare

Of Perfume shall fling up into the Air,

As not a True Believer passing by

But shall be overtaken unaware.

LXIX

Indeed, the Idols I have loved so long

Have done my Credit in Men's Eye much wrong:

Have drown'd my Honour in a shallow Cup,

And sold my Reputation for a Song.

LXX

Indeed, indeed, Repentance oft before

I swore—but was I sober when I swore?

    And then and then came Spring, and Rose-in-
        hand

My thread-bare Penitence a-pieces tore.

LXXI

And much as Wine has play'd the Infidel,

And robb'd me of my Robe of Honour—well,

I often wonder what the Vintners buy

One half so precious as the Goods they sell.

LXXII

Alas, that Spring should vanish with the Rose!

That Youth's sweet - scented Manuscript should
close!

The Nightingale that in the Branches sang,

Ah, whence, and whither flown again, who knows!

LXXIII

Ah, Moon of my Delight who know'st no wane,

The Moon of Heav'n is rising once again:

How oft hereafter rising shall she look

Through this same Garden after me—in vain!

LXXIV

Ah, Love! could thou and I with Fate conspire

To grasp this sorry Scheme of Things entire,

    Would not we shatter it to bits—and then

Re-mould it nearer to the Heart's Desire!

LXXV

And when Thyself with shining Foot shall pass

Among the Guests Star-scatter'd on The Grass,

    And in Thy joyous Errand reach the Spot

Where I made one—turn down an empty Glass!

TAMÁM SHUD.

EDMUND·J·SULLIVAN.

RUBÁIYÁT

OF

OMAR KHAYYÁM.

I.

Wake! For the Sun, who scatter'd into flight
The Stars before him from the Field of Night,
   Drives Night along with them from Heav'n, and
      strikes
The Sultán's Turret with a Shaft of Light.

II.

Before the phantom of False morning died,
Methought a Voice within the Tavern cried,
   "When all the Temple is prepared within,
"Why nods the drowsy Worshiper outside?"

III.

And, as the Cock crew, those who stood before
The Tavern shouted—"Open then the Door!
   "You know how little while we have to stay,
And, once departed, may return no more."

Now the New Year reviving old Desires,
The thoughtful Soul to Solitude retires,
    Where the WHITE HAND OF MOSES on the Bough
Puts out, and Jesus from the Ground suspires.

Iram indeed is gone with all his Rose,
And Jamshyd's Sev'n-ring'd Cup where no one knows;
    But still a Ruby kindles in the Vine,
And many a Garden by the Water blows.

And David's lips are lockt; but in divine
High-piping Pehleví, with "Wine! Wine! Wine!
    "Red Wine!"—the Nightingale cries to the Rose
That sallow cheek of hers to' incarnadine.

Come, fill the Cup, and in the fire of Spring
Your Winter garment of Repentance fling:
    The Bird of Time has but a little way
To flutter—and the Bird is on the Wing.

Whether at Naishápúr or Babylon,
Whether the Cup with sweet or bitter run,
    The Wine of Life keeps oozing drop by drop,
The Leaves of Life keep falling one by one

IX.

Each Morn a thousand Roses brings, you say:
Yes, but where leaves the Rose of Yesterday?
    And this first Summer month that brings the Rose
Shall take Jamshyd and Kaikobád away.

X.

Well, let it take them! What have we to do
With Kaikobád the Great, or Kaikhosrú?
    Let Zál and Rustum bluster as they will,
Or Hátim call to Supper—heed not you.

XI.

With me along the strip of Herbage strown
That just divides the desert from the sown,
    Where name of Slave and Sultán is forgot—
And Peace to Mahmúd on his golden Throne!

XII.

A Book of Verses underneath the Bough,
A Jug of Wine, a Loaf of Bread—and Thou
    Beside me singing in the Wilderness—
Oh, Wilderness were Paradise enow!

XIII.

Some for the Glories of This World; and some
Sigh for the Prophet's Paradise to come;
    Ah, take the Cash, and let the Credit go,
Nor heed the rumble of a distant Drum!

XIV.

Look to the blowing Rose about us—"Lo,
Laughing," she says, "into the world I blow,
  At once the silken tassel of my Purse
Tear, and its Treasure on the Garden throw."

XV.

And those who husbanded the Golden grain,
And those who flung it to the winds like Rain,
  Alike to no such aureate Earth are turn'd
As, buried once, Men want dug up again.

XVI.

The Worldly Hope men set their Hearts upon
Turns Ashes—or it prospers; and anon,
  Like Snow upon the Desert's dusty Face,
Lighting a little hour or two—is gone.

XVII.

Think, in this batter'd Caravanserai
Whose Portals are alternate Night and Day,
  How Sultán after Sultán with his Pomp
Abode his destined Hour, and went his way.

XVIII.

They say the Lion and the Lizard keep
The courts where Jamshyd gloried and drank deep:
  And Bahrám, that great Hunter—the Wild Ass
Stamps o'er his Head, but cannot break his Sleep.

XIX

I sometimes think that never blows so red
The Rose as where some buried Cæsar bled;
  That every Hyacinth the Garden wears
Dropt in her Lap from some once lovely Head.

XX.

And this reviving Herb whose tender Green
Fledges the River-Lip on which we lean—
  Ah, lean upon it lightly! for who knows
From what once lovely Lip it springs unseen!

XXI.

Ah, my Belovéd, fill the Cup that clears
To-DAY of past Regrets and future Fears:
  To-morrow—Why, To-morrow I may be
Myself with Yesterday's Sev'n thousand Years.

XXII.

For some we loved, the loveliest and the best
That from his Vintage rolling Time hath prest,
  Have drunk their Cup a Round or two before,
And one by one crept silently to rest.

XXIII.

And we, that now make merry in the Room
They left, and Summer dresses in new bloom,
  Ourselves must we beneath the Couch of Earth
Descend—ourselves to make a Couch—for whom?

Ah, make the most of what we yet may spend,
Before we too into the Dust descend;
  Dust into Dust, and under Dust to lie,
Sans Wine, sans Song, sans Singer, and—sans End!

Alike for those who for To-DAY prepare,
And those that after some To-MORROW stare,
  A Muezzín from the Tower of Darkness cries,
"Fools! your Reward is neither Here nor There."

Why, all the Saints and Sages who discuss'd
Of the Two Worlds so wisely—they are thrust
  Like foolish Prophets forth; their Words to Scorn
Are scatter'd, and their Mouths are stopt with Dust.

Myself when young did eagerly frequent
Doctor and Saint, and heard great argument
  About it and about: but evermore
Came out by the same door where in I went.

With them the seed of Wisdom did I sow,
And with mine own hand wrought to make it grow;
  And this was all the Harvest that I reap'd—
"I came like Water, and like Wind I go."

Into this Universe, and *Why* not knowing
Nor *Whence,* like Water willy-nilly flowing;
   And out of it, as Wind along the Waste,
I know not *Whither,* willy-nilly blowing.

What, without asking, hither hurried *Whence?*
And, without asking, *Whither* hurried hence!
   Oh, many a Cup of this forbidden Wine
Must drown the memory of that insolence!

Up from Earth's Center through the Seventh Gate
I rose, and on the Throne of Saturn sate,
   And many a Knot unravel'd by the Road;
But not the Master-knot of Human Fate.

There was the Door to which I found no Key;
There was the Veil through which I might not see:
   Some little talk awhile of ME and THEE
There was—and then no more of THEE and ME.

Earth could not answer; nor the Seas that mourn
In flowing Purple, of their Lord Forlorn;
   Nor rolling Heaven, with all his Signs reveal'd
And hidden by the sleeve of Night and Morn.

XXXIV.

Then of the THEE IN ME who works behind
The Veil, I lifted up my hands to find
   A lamp amid the Darkness; and I heard,
As from Without—"THE ME WITHIN THEE BLIND!"

XXXV.

Then to the Lip of this poor earthen Urn
I lean'd, the Secret of my Life to learn:
   And Lip to Lip it murmur'd—"While you live,
"Drink!—for, once dead, you never shall return."

XXXVI.

I think the Vessel, that with fugitive
Articulation answer'd, once did live,
   And drink; and Ah! the passive Lip I kiss'd,
How many Kisses might it take—and give!

XXXVII.

For I remember stopping by the way
To watch a Potter thumping his wet Clay:
   And with its all-obliterated Tongue
It murmur'd—"Gently, Brother, gently, pray!"

XXXVIII.

And has not such a Story from of Old
Down Man's successive generations roll'd
   Of such a clod of saturated Earth
Cast by the Maker into Human mold?

And not a drop that from our Cups we throw
For Earth to drink of, but may steal below
   To quench the fire of Anguish in some Eye
There hidden—far beneath, and long ago.

As then the Tulip for her morning sup
Of Heav'nly Vintage from the soil looks up,
   Do you devoutly do the like, till Heav'n
To Earth invert you—like an empty Cup.

Perplext no more with Human or Divine,
To-morrow's tangle to the winds resign,
   And lose your fingers in the tresses of
The Cypress-slender Minister of Wine.

And if the Wine you drink, the Lip you press,
End in what All begins and ends in—Yes;
   Think then you are To-day what Yesterday
You were—To-morrow you shall not be less.

So when that Angel of the darker Drink
At last shall find you by the river-brink,
   And, offering his Cup, invite your Soul
Forth to your Lips to quaff—you shall not shrink.

Why, if the Soul can fling the Dust aside,
And naked on the Air of Heaven ride,
    Were't not a Shame—were't not a Shame for him
In this clay carcass crippled to abide?

'Tis but a Tent where takes his one day's rest
A Sultán to the realm of Death addrest;
    The Sultán rises, and the dark Ferrash
Strikes, and prepares it for another Guest.

And fear not lest Existence closing your
Account, and mine, should know the like no more;
    The Eternal Sákí from that Bowl has pour'd
Millions of Bubbles like us, and will pour.

When You and I behind the Veil are past,
Oh, but the long, long while the World shall last,
    Which of our Coming and Departure heeds
As the Sea's self should heed a pebble-cast.

A Moment's Halt—a momentary taste
Of BEING from the Well amid the Waste—
    And Lo!—the phantom Caravan has reach'd
The NOTHING it set out from—Oh, make haste!

Would you that spangle of Existence spend
About THE SECRET—quick about it, Friend!
    A Hair perhaps divides the False from True—
And upon what, prithee, may life depend?

A Hair perhaps divides the False and True;
Yes; and a single Alif were the clue—
    Could you but find it—to the Treasure-house,
And peradventure to THE MASTER too;

Whose secret Presence through Creation's veins
Running Quicksilver-like eludes your pains;
    Taking all shapes from Máh to Máhi and
They change and perish all—but He remains;

A moment guessed—then back behind the Fold
Immerst of Darkness round the Drama roll'd
    Which, for the Pastime of Eternity,
He doth Himself contrive, enact, behold.

But if in vain, down on the stubborn floor
Of Earth, and up to Heav'n's unopening Door,
    You gaze TO-DAY, while You are You—how then
TO-MORROW, when You shall be You no more?

Waste not your Hour, nor in the vain pursuit
Of This and That endeavor and dispute;
   Better be jocund with the fruitful Grape
Than sadden after none, or bitter, Fruit.

You know, my Friends, with what a brave Carouse
I made a Second Marriage in my house;
   Divorced old barren Reason from my Bed,
And took the Daughter of the Vine to Spouse.

For "Is" and "Is-not" though with Rule and Line
And "Up-and-down" by Logic I define,
   Of all that one should care to fathom, I
Was never deep in anything but—Wine.

Ah, by my Computations, People say,
Reduce the Year to better reckoning?—Nay,
   'Twas only striking from the Calendar
Unborn To-morrow and dead Yesterday.

And lately, by the Tavern Door agape,
Came shining through the Dusk an Angel Shape
   Bearing a Vessel on his Shoulder; and
He bid me taste of it; and 'twas—the Grape!

LIX.

The Grape that can with Logic absolute
The Two-and-Seventy jarring Sects confute:
    The sovereign Alchemist that in a trice
Life's leaden metal into Gold transmute;

LX.

The mighty Mahmúd, Allah-breathing Lord,
That all the misbelieving and black Horde
    Of Fears and Sorrows that infest the Soul
Scatters before him with his whirlwind Sword.

LXI.

Why, be this Juice the growth of God, who dare
Blaspheme the twisted tendril as a Snare?
    A Blessing, we should use it, should we not?
And if a Curse—why, then, Who set it there?

LXII.

I must abjure the Balm of Life, I must,
Scared by some After-reckoning ta'en on trust,
    Or lured with Hope of some Diviner Drink,
To fill the Cup—when crumbled into Dust!

LXIII.

Of threats of Hell and Hopes of Paradise!
One thing at least is certain—*This* Life flies;
    One thing is certain and the rest is Lies;
The Flower that once has blown for ever dies.

LXIV.

Strange, is it not? that of the myriads who
Before us pass'd the door of Darkness through,
  Not one returns to tell us of the Road,
Which to discover we must travel too.

LXV.

The Revelations of Devout and Learn'd
Who rose before us, and as Prophets burn'd,
  Are all but Stories, which, awoke from Sleep
They told their comrades, and to Sleep return'd.

LXVI.

I sent my Soul through the Invisible,
Some letter of that After-life to spell:
  And by and by my Soul return'd to me,
And answer'd "I Myself am Heav'n and Hell:"

LXVII.

Heav'n but the Vision of fulfill'd Desire,
And Hell the Shadow from a Soul on fire,
  Cast on the Darkness into which Ourselves,
So late emerged from, shall so soon expire.

LXVIII.

We are no other than a moving row
Of Magic Shadow-shapes that come and go
  Round with the Sun-illumined Lantern held
In Midnight by the Master of the Show;

LXIX.

But helpless Pieces of the Game He plays
Upon this Chequer-board of Nights and Days;
   Hither and thither moves, and checks, and slays,
And one by one back in the Closet lays.

LXX.

The Ball no question makes of Ayes and Noes,
But Here or There as strikes the Player goes;
   And He that toss'd you down into the Field,
He knows about it all—HE knows—HE knows!

LXXI.

The Moving Finger writes; and, having writ,
Moves on: nor all your Piety nor Wit
   Shall lure it back to cancel half a Line,
Nor all your Tears wash out a Word of it.

LXXII.

And that inverted Bowl they call the Sky,
Whereunder crawling coop'd we live and die,
   Lift not your hands to *It* for help—for It
As impotently moves as you or I.

LXXIII.

With Earth's first Clay They did the Last Man knead,
And there of the Last Harvest sow'd the Seed:
   And the first Morning of Creation wrote
What the Last Dawn of Reckoning shall read.

YESTERDAY *This* Day's Madness did prepare;
TO-MORROW's Silence, Triumph, or Despair:
 Drink! for you not know whence you came, nor why:
Drink! for you know not why you go nor where.

I tell you this—When, started from the Goal,
Over the flaming shoulders of the Foal
 Of Heav'n Parwín and Mushtarí they flung,
In my predestined Plot of Dust and Soul.

The Vine had struck a fiber: which about
It clings my Being—let the Dervish flout;
 Of my Base metal may be filed a Key
That shall unlock the Door he howls without.

And this I know: whether the one True Light
Kindle to Love, or Wrath-consume me quite,
 One Flash of It within the Tavern caught
Better than in the Temple lost outright.

What! out of senseless Nothing to provoke
A conscious Something to resent the yoke
 Of unpermitted Pleasure, under pain
Of Everlasting Penalties, if broke!

What! from his helpless Creature be repaid
Pure Gold for what he lent him dross-allay'd—
   Sue for a Debt he never did contract,
And cannot answer—Oh the sorry trade!

Oh Thou, who didst with pitfall and with gin
Beset the Road I was to wander in,
   Thou wilt not with Predestined Evil round
Enmesh, and then impute my Fall to Sin!

Oh Thou, who Man of baser Earth didst make,
And ev'n with Paradise devise the Snake:
   For all the Sin wherewith the Face of Man
Is blacken'd—Man's forgiveness give—and take!

*   *   *   *   *   *

As under cover of departing Day
Slunk hunger-stricken Ramazán away,
   Once more within the Potter's house alone
I stood, surrounded by the Shapes of Clay.

Shapes of all Sorts and Sizes, great and small,
That stood along the floor and by the wall;
   And some loquacious Vessels were; and some
Listen'd perhaps, but never talk'd at all.

Said one among them—"Surely not in vain
My substance of the common Earth was ta'en
   And to this Figure molded, to be broke,
Or trampled back to shapeless Earth again."

Then said a Second—"Ne'er a peevish Boy
Would break the Bowl from which he drank in joy:
   And He that with his hand the Vessel made
Will surely not in after Wrath destroy."

After a momentary silence spake
Some Vessel of a more ungainly Make;
   "They sneer at me for leaning all awry:
What! did the Hand then of the Potter shake?"

Whereat some one of the loquacious Lot—
I think a Súfi pipkin—waxing hot—
   "All this of Pot and Potter—Tell me then,
Who is the Potter, pray, and who the Pot?"

"Why," said another, "Some there are who tell
Of one who threatens he will toss to Hell
   The luckless Pots he marr'd in making—Pish!
He's a Good Fellow, and 'twill all be well."

"Well," murmured one, "Let whoso make or buy,
My Clay with long Oblivion is gone dry:
    But fill me with the old familiar Juice,
Methinks I might recover by and by."

XC.

So while the Vessels one by one were speaking,
The little Moon look'd in that all were seeking:
    And then they jogg'd each other, "Brother! Brother!
Now for the Porter's shoulders' knot a-creaking!"

*　　*　　*　　*　　*　　*

XCI.

Ah, with the Grape my fading life provide,
And wash the Body whence the Life has died,
    And lay me, shrouded in the living Leaf,
By some not unfrequented Garden-side.

XCII.

That ev'n buried Ashes such a snare
Of Vintage shall fling up into the Air
    As not a True-believer passing by
But shall be overtaken unaware.

XCIII.

Indeed the Idols I have loved so long
Have done my credit in this World much wrong:
    Have drown'd my Glory in a shallow Cup,
And sold my reputation for a Song.

Indeed, indeed, Repentance oft before
I swore—but was I sober when I swore?
    And then and then came Spring, and Rose-in-hand
My thread-bare Penitence apieces tore.

And much as Wine has play'd the Infidel,
And robb'd me of my Robe of Honor—Well,
    I wonder often what the Vintners buy
One half so precious as the stuff they sell.

Yet Ah, that Spring should vanish with the Rose!
That Youth's sweet-scented manuscript should close!
    The Nightingale that in the branches sang,
Ah whence, and whither flown again, who knows!

Would but the Desert of the Fountain yield
One glimpse—if dimly, yet indeed, reveal'd,
    To which the fainting Traveler might spring,
As springs the trampled herbage of the field!

Would but some wingéd Angel ere too late
Arrest the yet unfolded Roll of Fate,
    And make the stern Recorder otherwise
Enregister, or quite obliterate!

Ah Love! could you and I with Him conspire
To grasp this sorry Scheme of Things entire,
    Would not we shatter it to bits—and then
Re-mold it nearer to the Heart's Desire!

*   *   *   *   *   *

C.

Yon rising Moon that looks for us again—
How oft hereafter will she wax and wane;
    How oft hereafter rising look for us
Through this same Garden—and for *one* in vain!

CI.

And when like her, oh Sákí, you shall pass
Among the Guests Star-scatter'd on the Grass,
    And in your joyous errand reach the spot
Where I made One—turn down an empty Glass!

TAMAM.